VideoWorkshop

for

Introduction to Communication
Student Learning Guide with CD-ROM

prepared by

Edward Lee Lamoureux
Bradley University

Boston   New York   San Francisco
Mexico City   Montreal   Toronto   London   Madrid   Munich   Paris
Hong Kong   Singapore   Tokyo   Cape Town   Sydney

ISBN 0-205-37805-6

Printed in the United States of America

10 9 8 7   08 07 06 05 04 03

Student Learning Guide
Table of Contents

Explanatory Note for Using This Book

Many of the activities in this book refer to the video segments contained on the CD-ROM. For example, a section reads: "Between 5 and 6, Sarah's roommate says that Patrick said that he didn't like Sarah's presentation." Each video features a numeric bar, like the one shown, just below the video display box. The bar is numbered 1-7 and these are the numbers referred to in phrases such as "Between 5 and 6."

Unit One
Communication Principles
Communication is an Irreversible Process

Objectives

The ideas that communication is a process and that it is irreversible are conceptual and sometimes difficult to see concretely. The example illustrates some of the difficulties. Focus on Emily's attempt to "take a saying back."

- Note the nature of communication as an ongoing process that always moves forward.
- Focus on the effects of trying to take communication back, of trying to reverse the process.
- Learn to craft alternate responses in situations when "reversing communication" is not possible.

Review

Communication transactions are spiral-like, rather than linear and sequential. Once created, communication has the physical property of matter; it can't be uncreated. After you say something (or enact a nonverbal message), you can't "take it back," though subsequent things you say and do can modify meanings. And of course, trying to clarify will sometimes increase the damage from the initial communication. As a process, communication is ongoing and influences all aspects of the sender, receiver, message, and situation complex.

Video

Emily and Jared are at a key point in their troubled relationship. Perhaps they will put their differences aside and stay together. But Emily's effort to block the effects of her talk fails.

Observations

Emily, in her frustration with the situation and conflict at hand, makes a comment that could hurt Jared's feelings, thereby further damaging their relationship and complicating the situation. She wants to "take it back." But of course, she cannot.

- Note the ways in which Emily's saying, at 3, tries to "take back" a hurtful comment ("Get a grip.").

- Recognize the degree to which her attempt is ineffective.

- What are the outcomes of the unsuccessful attempt to get Jared to ignore the saying?

_____

_____

_____

_____

Next Step

While it would be easy to say that the best thing Emily could have done was to have not made the "get a grip" comment in the first place, let's assume that the comment has been made.

Rewrite her next words to reflect a better solution for the problems the comment might raise. Explain the reasons behind the approach you took to the repair.

_____

_____

_____

_____

Quiz

1. The increased use of electronic communication, especially computer mediated messages such as electronic mail
   a. has no effect on the process of communication as irreversible.
   b. increases the degree to which the process of communication is reversible.
   c. decreases the degree to which the process of communication is irreversible.
   d. increases the degree to which the process of communication is irreversible.

   _____

2. The model of communication that is most compliant with the view of communication as an irreversible process is the
   a. interactional model of communication.
   b. transactional model of communication.
   c. linear model of communication.
   d. all of the above.

   _____

3. Divorce is a good example showing that the process of communication between two people can end, especially when the outcome of their relationship is negative.
   TRUE   FALSE

   _____

Web

The Infinity Foundation was created in New Jersey, in 1994, by a private endowment. The Foundation is a private non-operating foundation that provides grants to nonprofit organizations for charitable, holistic healing, scientific, religious, or educational purposes. A special emphasis is creating, disseminating, and expanding a body of knowledge that clarifies or integrates philosophy, religion, science, psychology, and non-traditional mystical disciplines, thereby bridging Eastern philosophies with Western thought.

Student Learning Guide

To that end, Ramesh N. Rao presented: "Beyond Mass Communication: A Communication Studies Agenda for India" at The Indira Gandhi National Center for the Arts on June 14, 2001.

Through this paper/presentation, you can learn how teaching basic principles of communication study (including "communication is irreversible") could well serve as a way to improve education in other countries and traditions as in this case in India:

http://www.infinityfoundation.com/mandala/s_es/s_es_rao-r_agenda.htm

Unit Two
Communication and the Self
Communication and Self-Concept

Objectives

Some factors in self-concept development focus on activities associated with the evaluations and responses of others. Some factors focus on the person and her/his self-awareness and evaluations.

- Recognize and identify the behaviors through which Kathy displays her self-concept and factors of its development.
- Note the ways in which others challenge and influence self-concept.
- Identify relationships between self-concept and the attitudes, beliefs, and values Kathy communicates.

Review

Self-concept is an ever-changing process of how you perceive yourself: your feelings and thoughts about your strengths and weaknesses, your abilities and limitations. It is based on your self-awareness of your identity and is expressed via your subjective descriptions of who you think you are and how you see yourself as a person.

Self-concept develops from communication with others, our associations with groups, the roles we assume, the image others have of you (looking glass self), comparisons between yourself and others (social comparison), your cultural experiences (particularly gender roles and the influences of ethnicity and socio-economic factors), your own self evaluations and labels, and the various ways that others respond to you and your behavior.

Your self concept is reflected in the attitudes, beliefs, and values you hold.

Video

Kathy appears very clear about the relationships between her self-concept and the name she will use after marriage. Her friends differ over the issue. What effects do their opinions have on Kathy's self-concept? Why?

Observations

- Between 4 and 5, Kathy notes a number of factors that contribute to her sense of self. What are they? Are they primarily based on self-evaluations or evaluations by others?

_____

_____

- Between 6 and 7, Kathy shows a different set of factors. What are they? Do they support or undermine her previously articulated sense of self?

_____

_____

- Which attitudes, beliefs, and values appear to be most evident in Kathy's talk?

_____

_____

Next Step

- Write a response for Kathy, between 3 and 4, that is a direct defense of her self-concept, rather than a more general statement of her views on the situation.

_____

_____

- Could Kathy's friends question the wisdom of her planned name change without seeming to attack her self-concept? What might they say?

_____

_____

Quiz

1. Which factor of self-concept is most crucial?
   a. cultural teachings
   b. significant others' images of you
   c. your self-interpretations and evaluations
   d. your social comparisons with others
   e. all of the above

   _____

2.   Factors that influence self-concept in childhood have the same influence later in life.
        TRUE   FALSE

        _____

3.   Select the correct saying
        a. Our attitudes shape our behavior, but not our core self-concept.
        b. Looking to others to help us define our self-concept is generally a mistake.
        c. Communicating cross-culturally can change assumptions about self-concepts.

        _____

Web

        Communication in new media environments promises to present interesting challenges to what we know about identity development. Communication professor Mark Giese published an article that examines how people represent themselves in online interactions in "electronic communities."

        "Self without Body: Textual Self-Representation in an Electronic Community," published in *First Monday*, a peer-reviewed internet journal:

        http://www.firstmonday.dk/issues/issue3_4/giese/

Unit Three
Communication and the Self
Communicating Self-Esteem

Objectives

Self-esteem is one of the primary components of self-concept. Self-esteem deals with emotions (how we feel about ourselves), so interactions with other people involving our self-esteem can be "charged" events.

- Notice the way that Kathy's expressions of feelings for herself influence the ways she responds to gender expectations.
- Notice the way that Kathy's expressions of feelings for herself influence the ways she responds to conflict.
- Note that when her friend challenges Kathy's decision about changing her name, the conflict that emerges could damage Kathy's self-esteem. Does it?

Review

Self-esteem refers to the way you feel about yourself—how much you like yourself, how valuable a person you think you are, how competent you think you are. Your feelings and attitudes about yourself reflect the value you place on yourself. Your self-esteem can reflect your daily view of yourself.

Video

Kathy appears to have a strong and positive self-esteem. The conversation raises issues about her decision and challenges some of her attitudes, beliefs, and values about identity work.

Observations

- At a number of points, one of Kathy's male friends "makes fun" of her married name (Fudd). How does she respond to his suggestions? Does her response support her self-esteem? How so?

9

- At 6, Kathy's friend is very emphatic over the seriousness of the challenge to Kathy's identity posed by the proposed name change. How does Kathy's response treat the perceived threat?

_____

_____

Next Step

- Either in a small group discussion, or as a thought paper you write, discuss the implications to self-esteem brought about by traditions surrounding names after marriage. List the "standard" American options; consider the implications to both parties in the union.

_____

_____

- Investigate and describe the post-marriage naming practices in a tradition that is different than the "standard" American mode in which the woman keeps her "given" name and changes her "family" name.

_____

_____

Quiz

1. Self-esteem is
    a. our mental picture of ourselves or our social identity.
    b. made up of beliefs that prevent you from building meaningful relationships.
    c. the human ability to think about what we're doing while we're doing it.
    d. the picture you have of yourself in a particular situation.
    e. none of the above.

    _____

2. High self-esteem, in general American culture, is associated with the fulfillment of qualities ascribed to gender (e.g., independence for men, connectedness for women).
    TRUE   FALSE

    _____

3. Nuturing people
    a. are to be avoided, as they can damage your self-esteem.
    b. are especially helpful at those times when your self-esteem is damaged.
    c. will engage in "pity parties" that will help you alter negative behaviors.
    d. all of the above.

    _____

Web

On the Valdosa State University Web site, Dr. William Huitt and others feature a number of topics related to their interests in educational psychology:

http://chiron.valdosta.edu/whuitt/edpsyindx.html

On this page, self-esteem and self-concept are defined and discussed. Additional references are provided:

http://chiron.valdosta.edu/whuitt/col/regsys/self.html

Unit Four
Communication and the Self
Self-Disclosure in Interpersonal Communciation

Objectives

Self-disclosure is a complex phenomena that is strongly related to the development of interpersonal relationships. Communicators manage a number of features when involved in self-disclosive transactions. To better understand it, you should be able to:

- Differentiate between:
  - ➢ talk that is only marginally self-disclosive.
  - ➢ talk that discloses important, and sometimes personal, information that is not directly about self.
  - ➢ talk that is self-disclosive of feelings.
- Appreciate the value to interpersonal relationship development of the reciprocal nature of self-disclosure.

Review

Self-disclosure is the sharing of information about ourselves that others are not likely to know. Self-disclosures can be either voluntary (conscious) or involuntary (slips of the tongue). Self-disclosure reveals personal information at various levels of intimacy, ranging from relatively straightforward references to your attitudes, beliefs, values, and behaviors to the sharing of your intimate feelings about self. Because people close to you play important roles in your life, sometimes discussing matters about them is self-disclosure. However, common gossip about others is not considered self-disclosure. As relationships develop, self-disclosure often increases in intimacy. Since self-disclosure (deciding to do it and living with the results) is based on trust, it is often gradually reciprocal.

Video

Jamie's friend, Emma, has some serious news to share. It takes some time for the two of them to work up to the really important information, but as they interact, we learn a lot about their relationship.

Observations

- Note the way that small talk is used in "self-disclosure-like" ways. At 2, Jamie and Emma share information about dorm food and a mutual friend in ways that are not really self-disclosive.

- Just after 2, Emma discloses her mother's medical condition. Notice how talk about another person can be self-disclosive. Emma doesn't share self-disclosures about her feelings until after 6. Note when she shifts to personal information about self.

- Chart the points at which the conversation features reciprocal and gradual escalation of self-disclosures.

Next Step

Jamie asked Emma for details about Emma's mother's illness and listened intently. This focus was important. However, Jamie did not, at any point, inquire as to Emma's feelings over the situation. Likewise, though Emma detailed her mother's situation in a disclosive way, she barely talked about her feelings.

Re-write their dialogue from just after 2, when Emma discloses her mother's medical condition. However, craft appropriate and effective ways for both women to seek information about Emma's feelings.

_____

_____

_____

_____

Quiz

1. Men usually self-disclose about activities and interests, rather than about feelings. This means that their relationships do not develop meaningfully.
   TRUE   FALSE

   _____

2. Select the correct statement
   a. Self-disclosure should be used as a way to get our friends to tell us secrets about other acquaintances.
   b. Self-disclosure only "counts" if it is about our inner most feelings.
   c. The best time for intimate self-disclosures is early in relationships.
   d. None of the above.

   _____

3.   Explain how self-disclosure during relationship development may be described, by using the analogy of an onion and its skin.

_____

_____

_____

Web

     Allyn & Bacon's *Communication Studies* Web site offers useful information and activities. Find there a unit on self-disclosure that includes definitions, concept discussions, a quick quiz, and an interactive activity:

     http://www.abacon.com/commstudies/interpersonal/indisclosure.html

Unit Five
Perception
Effective Perception Checking

Objectives

Perception is a universal, yet individual, process. Each person experiences and interprets the world somewhat differently from others. Clarifying your perceptions, aligning these with others, and noting perceptual differences are important for effective communication.

- Learn to validate perception-based assumptions by asking questions about your observations and interpretations and those of others.
- Note the difference between describing external events and internal interpretations.
- Practice formulating "perception checks" that offer others opportunities to help you clarify meanings.

Review

Perception is a process through which humans attend to, select, organize, interpret, and remember stimulating phenomena. Although all people are constantly involved in perception and aspects of the process are sometimes similar across individuals (especially among closely related members of families or cultural groups), each person perceives the world in unique ways that are open to a number of influences. It is difficult for us to know what and how each other perceives. Making our perceptions clear to others is an important part of effective communication and mutual understanding.

Through perception checking, we give others access to descriptions of what we think we've experienced (we describe the stimuli) and to our interpretations (we describe our feelings). Then we offer them an opportunity to correct us, to add their interpretations, or to validate our perceptions.

Video

Jamie and Dave, initially, do not agree as to how much work and time they should put into their joint project. As they talk, they clarify perceptions of the importance of and their motivations for the activity.

Observations

- At 2, Dave asks Jamie about her grades and scores. He then reveals his, by comparison. Note how Jamie struggles seeing the relevance of Dave's attempt at displaying his perception of the situation.

- Just before 4, Jamie gets Dave to check her perception about Dr. Smith's grading procedures. Notice how she includes a description of what she has observed, as well as describing how she feels about the stimuli.

- Note Dave's response to Jamie's perception. Is it validation or contradiction? Why?

_____

_____

Next step

Complete the following rewrite of a portion of their conversation in a way that produces clear and efficient perception checks.

Jamie:

(Describes the behavioral stimuli): Dave, it looks to me that you are:

_____

_____

(Describes her feelings): When you do this, I:

_____

_____

Jamie, continued:

    (Checks the perception):

_____

_____

Dave:
    (Describes the behavioral stimuli): Well Jamie, it sounds to me like you are:

_____

_____

    (Describes his feelings): When you say this, I:

_____

_____

(Checks the perception):

_____

_____

Quiz

1. You should always check your perceptions directly with the person to whom you are speaking. Avoid indirect perception checking.
    TRUE   FALSE

    _____

2. The purpose(s) for perception checking is to
    a. check the accuracy of your perceptions and attributions.
    b. reduce uncertainty by further exploring others' thoughts and feelings.
    c. help you sharpen your initial perception toward accuracy.
    d. all of the above.

    _____

3. Select the correct statement
    a. Perception is a function of the situation and the people's behavior we are perceiving.
    b. Evaluations should be made as soon as possible after initial impressions; first impressions are best.
    c. Personal biases seldom interfere with perception.
    d. None of the above.

    _____

Web

The Institute for Management Excellence offers practical tools for business and corporate clients and publishes an online newsletter. The August 1997 issue provides practical information for improving verbal skills, particularly "Listening Skills–A key element to learning to communicate well" which provides exercises and examples of perception checking:

http://www.itstime.com/aug97a.htm

Unit Six
Verbal Communication
Meaning: Denotation and Connotation

Objectives

Verbal communication presents a paradox—meanings are determined by the complex inter-mixing of widely shared conventions with personal and idiosyncratic practices. This unit will help you clarify important distinctions between taken-for-granted linguistic assumptions and meaning-in-use by asking you to:

- Note the differences in a communication scene between the denotative and connotative meanings of words.
- Recognize implications to relationships and interactions that can be caused by differences in meanings.
- Notice how people attempt to use connotative meanings as though they are denotative.

Review

Words have connotative and denotative meanings. Denotation is the generally accepted "dictionary" definition through which words are taken to be literal and about content. People who use a word usually know its denotative meaning.

However, when we actually use words, we are also using their connotative meanings, perhaps even more so than denotation. Connotation refers to the personal and subjective meanings each person has for words and sayings. Connotative meaning communicates much of language's emotional content.

Video

Sarah's eagerly awaited date, Patrick, has either said that "he is really interested" in Sarah or that he "finds her interesting." These words, "interested" and "interesting," are, well, interesting.

Observations

Sarah's roommate revealed that the intended date did not like Sarah's class presentation. At 4, Sarah notes that her roommate told her that Patrick is "really interested" in her. Just before 6, Sarah discovers that, in spite of other factors, her date finds her "interesting."

- Sarah uses the term, "really interested in me," while Sarah's roommate uses the term, "finds you interesting," as though they both know what each means–denotatively. What is meant by each terms' denotative meaning?

_____

_____

- What connotative meaning does Sarah attach to the term her roommate uses in this context?

_____

_____

- What connotative meaning does Sarah's roommate attach to the term she uses?

_____

_____

Next Step

Write dialogue for Sarah's roommate that follows Sarah's saying at 4. Use the talk to clarify the situation by investigating what Sarah meant in her thinking that "Patrick is really interested in me." As part of the talk, clarify the mistaken assumption about Patrick's feelings toward the class presentation and his subsequent continued interest in dating Sarah.

_____

_____

_____

_____

_____

Quiz

1. A group of people get together and publish a manual of terms related to the highly technical work that they do. The purpose of the manual is to define the terms they often use on the job, especially for clients and other outsiders with and for whom they work. This effort is an attempt to
    a. further develop the connotative nature of their specialized language usages.
    b. build on language's facility for denotation.
    c. make it more difficult for "outsiders" to understand the ways the group speaks.
    d. improve the abstract nature of denotation to increase the ability of denotative terms to work as technical language in their work.

    _____

2. When interactants carry on everyday conversations, they proceed as though all parties understand, generally, the talk. This assumption
    a. underscores the fact that denotation is the primary mode of meaning for everyday conversation.
    b. shows that misunderstanding does not often occur in everyday communication because it deals with very straightforward meanings.
    c. illustrates the paradox that we often use connotative meanings as though they are denotative in nature.
    d. all of the above.

    _____

3. As the number of people who agree over the connotative meaning of a word increases, the meaning of the word shifts toward denotation.
    TRUE   FALSE

    _____

24

Student Learning Guide

Web

Mick Underwood sponsors the *Communication, Cultural and Media Studies (CCMS)* Web site, a valuable resource featuring a wide range of information communication-related issues. In particular, there is an excellent section on meaning, including much about the nature of denotation:

http://www.cultsock.ndirect.co.uk/MUHome/cshtml/semiomean/meaning1.html

Unit Seven
Verbal Communication
Meaning: Concrete and Abstract Language

Objectives

Language can be about specific objects and actions in the world or be about concepts and interpretations. Learning language flexibility is a key verbal competency.

- Note the differences between concrete and abstract language.
- Be able to move sayings up and down the ladder of abstraction.
- Appreciate the benefits of concrete and abstract language.

Review

General Semanticists Alfred Korzybski and S. I. Hiyakawa fostered interest in the varying degrees of concreteness (abstraction) available for word use. Concrete words are used when speaking about specific things that can be pointed to or physically experienced. Communication using concrete words leaves little room for disagreement, and when there are differences of opinion, they can usually be solved by pointing to the specific object and its features. Abstract words are symbols for ideas, qualities, interpretations, and relationships. Their meanings depend on the experiences and intentions of the person using them. Effective communicators use both concrete and abstract language, but they do so in appropriately by matching the level of abstraction to needs of particular communication events.

Video

Sarah's roommate tells her that Patrick hated Sarah's presentation. But was it the presentation that he disliked? Or Sarah? Or something else?

Observations

- Between 4 and 5, Sarah's roommate says that "Patrick didn't really like your Heidegger presentation…in fact, he hated it." Is this saying concrete or abstract?

_____

_____

27

- Between 5 and 6, Sarah's roommate says that Patrick said, "I hate Heidegger; he's a Nazi." Is this saying concrete or abstract?

_____

- Which of the two sayings was more helpful in explaining Patrick's relative interest in Sarah? Explain your answer.

_____

_____

Next Step

Go to the URL below and complete the exercise then take the following saying from this unit through the abstraction ladder: Patrick didn't like Sarah's presentation.

http://cwabacon.pearsoned.com/bookbind/pubbooks/devito_ab/chapter5/deluxe.html

_____

_____

_____

_____

Quiz

1.   The distinction between concrete and abstract words is the same as the distinction between denotation and connotation.
TRUE   FALSE

_____

2.   When deciding between concrete and abstract words, communicators should
a. always use concrete language; otherwise, listeners are apt to misunderstand.
b. always use abstract language; otherwise, speakers will be plain and boring.
c. mix in some abstract language as a way to "spice up" talk that is otherwise concrete.
d. chose words based on situational requirements (for example, when precision is required, use concrete language; when connection with feelings is required, use abstract words).

_____

3.   Discuss the ways that pointing to specific objects is an illustration of how verbally "climbing down the abstraction ladder" works.

_____

_____

_____

Web

The Institute of General Semantics pursues the continued study of the ideas popularized by Alfred Korzybski and S.I. Hiyakawa. The site includes a section titled, "General Semantics Basic Formulations:"

http://www.general-semantics.org/

Unit Eight
Nonverbal Communication
The Nature of Nonverbal Communication

Objectives

Studying communication often means learning various things about speaking and listening. But sometimes, actions speak louder than words. Nonverbal communication makes crucial contributions to every communication transaction. You should be able to

- Identify subtle and obvious features of nonverbal communication in a given situation.
- Appreciate the contributions that factors of nonverbal communication make to verbal messages.
- Suggest meaningful changes to nonverbal behavior that contribute to improvements in communication effectiveness.

Review

Nonverbal communication is communication without spoken or written language. Nonverbal messages communicate meanings and work with verbal messages to metacommunicate or comment on the meanings we transact verbally.

Nonverbal communication is:
- culture bound (cultures have unique rules for displaying and interpreting nonverbal).
- difficult to interpret because it is ambiguous, abstract, and arbitrary; is continuous whenever people are together in.
- not linguistic (though sometimes we use the term "body language," nonverbal isn't "regular" enough to function like a language).
- multichanneled as nonverbal cues register on our senses from a number of sources simultaneously (though we can only interpret one at a time).
- a carrier of meanings that are situational (context is very important to nonverbal meanings).

Video

Kristen and Dave are focusing on their relationship. In the past, they've worked together and have been there for each other, but now things are changing.

31

Observations

Watch the clip from start until the black-out, at 4. The sound is off so you can concentrate on nonverbal features. Stop the player at the blackout and:

- Identify important body movements and label their types (illustrators, affect displays, regulators, adaptors, emblems).

_____

_____

_____

- List two other types of nonverbal communication that are important to this scene.

_____

_____

_____

- Indicate in what ways this scene shows nonverbal communication to be ambiguous, abstract, and/or arbitrary.

_____

_____

_____

Student Learning Guide

Now play the video from the black-out at 4 through the end; the scene will repeat, this time with sound. Answer questions 1-3 again and note the degree to which access to the language affects your reading of the nonverbal communication.

- Identify important body movements and label their types (illustrators, affect displays, regulators, adaptors, emblems).

_____

_____

_____

- List two other types of nonverbal communication that are important to this scene.

_____

_____

_____

- Indicate in what ways this scene shows nonverbal communciation to be ambiguous, abstract, and/or arbitrary.

_____

_____

_____

Next Step

"Block" the nonverbal factors again in this scene; that is, specify the changes in nonverbal behavior that each interactant would make under two conditions (each):

- He wants them to be together.

_____

_____

- He doesn't really want them to be together (though he talks like he does).

_____

_____

- She wants them to be together.

_____

_____

- She doesn't really want them to be together (though she talks like she does).

_____

_____

Student Learning Guide

Quiz

1. Saying that nonverbal communication is ambiguous means that
    a. nonverbal does not communicate, it only confuses.
    b. senders of nonverbal cannot control their communication behavior.
    c. single instances of nonverbal can be difficult to understand; complex sets of nonverbal can mislead and confuse receivers.
    d. interactants should avoid interpreting nonverbal communication.

    _____

2. In situations when the receiver finds the content in a verbal message to be ambiguous, the receiver is more likely to believe the nonverbal portion of the message than the verbal.
    TRUE   FALSE

    _____

3. Smiling combines which factors of nonverbal communication?

    _____   _____   _____

Web

Marvin Hecht, Ph. D. has collected a number of online resources for the study of nonverbal communication, including links to nonverbal scholars, labs, associations, and publishers:

http://www.geocities.com/marvin_hecht/nonverbal.html

Unit Nine
Interpersonal Communication
Gender Influences on Language Behavior

Objectives

Some research indicates gender differences in language use. There are times when women and men appear to communicate in ways that can be categorized as though men communicate one way, and women in another. However, not all people behave in ways that follow these descriptions; likewise, behavior is sometimes circumstantial. Research informing our understandings of interpersonal communication behavior enables us to make observations about behavioral regularities and tendencies; individuals may behave in consonance with the proposals, or may violate the assumptions of such findings.

This unit should help you recognize differences between Mike and Susanne's behavior and to consider whether those differences appear gender-stereotypic or whether their behavior varies from gender-based expectations. As a result of the unit, you should be able to:

- Identify who controls turns-at-talk and analyze how turn taking is controlled.
- Note who controls topics and identify the language/interaction behaviors used to accomplish that control.
- Identify which speaker is more direct and to list the ways in which direct communication is used. Likewise, you should be able to notice the use of indirect speech.

Review

You've learned that men often communicate to exchange information; communicate to report; speak to get things done; focus on the content level of meaning; lecture like an "expert"; use few cues indicating they are listening; interrupt often; change topics often, thereby controlling the topic of conversation; speak directly when communicating confidently and powerfully; speak indirectly when expressing weakness or revealing a problem.

You've learned that that women often communicate to connect with others; communicate to develop relationships; speak to develop rapport with others; focus on the relational level of meaning; listen like a follower; use many cues indicating they are listening; take short turns-at-talk; share the floor with others by speaking simultaneously and by talking about the topic-at-hand.

Video

Susanna and Mike have important things to say to each other. They have chosen to communicate with each other about their issues, rather than (for example) to use monologic forms (write the other a letter or e-mail). In conversation, men and women sometimes "get to the point" via different strategies. Note the verbal behaviors each use to advance their own perspective and to redirect the other's perspective.

Observations

- List the ways (between 2 and 3) that Mike "speaks like a man" by controlling the conversation.

_____

_____

- Between 4 and 5, Susanna focuses on the relational level of meaning. How does she accomplish this?

_____

_____

- Does Mike always speak in a gender stereotypic way? If not, at what point(s) does he speak otherwise?

_____

_____

Next Step

- Compose a more direct alternative to Susanna's opening dialogue (just before 2, beginning with "Mike, I was thinking that we need to talk").

_____

_____

- Write dialogue for Mike, substituting for what he says between 2 and 3, that encourages Susanna's talk, rather than interrupting and redirecting it.

_____

_____

_____

_____

_____

_____

Quiz

1.   An expressive orientation
    a. wants to get things done.
    b. focuses how we communicate, not why.
    c. fosters harmoneous relationships.
    d. focuses on talk's content dimension.

_____

2.   Stereotypically, in same-sex conversations, women communicate to report the details of activities; men to develop rapport with others.
        TRUE   FALSE

        _____

3.   Select the correct saying
        a. Women take more and longer turns than do men.
        b. Men usually connect with others' topics
        c. Women interrupt more than do men.
        d. Women display more listening cues than do men.

        _____

Web

        Professor Deborah Tannen, Ph. D., is one of the most influencial scholar-writers on relationships between gender and language. Her Georgetown University Web site includes links to bibliographic material and interviews:

        http://www.georgetown.edu/tannen/

Unit Ten
Interpersonal Communication
Verbal Management of Interpersonal Conflict

Objectives

Relational conflict sometimes spurs growth. Over time, however, recurrent conflict wears people down and makes relational dissolution more likely. Communication behaviors during conflicts can play an important role in keeping conflicts constructive.

- Evaluate conflicts as constructive or destructive so that situations needing intervention can be identified and transformed.
- Learn constructive communication behaviors for conflict management.
- Identify destructive communication behaviors in conflict situations.

Review

According to William Wilmot and Joyce Hocker, conflict is an expressed struggle between two or more interdependent parties who perceive incompatible goals, scarce resources, and interference from others in achieving goals. When it leads to outcomes that satisfy all parties, conflict can be constructive but when those involved feel injured and hateful as the result of coercive communication, conflict is destructive.

Conflict can be over content (objects, events, and people external to those involved) or over interactants' relationships.

Video

Kristen and Steve are unable to speak directly with each other about their relationship. It appears very difficult for each to see things from the others' perspective.

Observations

Steve and Kristen use their script writing as a "cover" for things they want to say to each other. Assume that the script they are writing actually represents them taking, in addition to the things they say to each other outside the script.

41

List the instances in which they use negative communication strategies, such as gunnysacking (using stored up grievances), face-detracting attacks (treating others as less than fully able), beltlining (hitting below the belt), and verbal aggressiveness (using talk to inflict psychological pain).

_____

_____

_____

_____

Next Step

Third parties are often "dragged into" relational conflicts as a way to raise otherwise delicate issues without talking about these directly. Doing so often ruins the communication climate for constructive talk about mutually-held problems or issues.

Between 3 and 4 Steve and Kristen conflict over her "involvement" with Philip. Write new dialog for this conversation that uses assertive and other-oriented communication to inquire into the status of that relationship and to uncover Steve and Kristen's feelings about her relationship with Philip.

_____

_____

_____

_____

Quiz

1. Relational conflict is destructive when parties leave the conflict feeling injured, and is constructive when one party comes out the clear winner.
    TRUE   FALSE

    _____

2. When we clearly describe the events or actions that are, in our view, producing conflict, we
    a. blurt out complaints and represent hostility so that the other knows we are upset.
    b. are accommodating to the needs of the other person in the conflict.
    c. respond to conflict in a cooperative way that can lead to productive conflict management.
    d. none of the above.

    _____

3. Physically or psychologically withdrawing from conflicts, a strategy that can produce mixed results for conflict management, is called

    _____

Web

The *Management Assistance Program for Nonprofits*, in Minneapolis/St. Paul, provides management assistance to nonprofit organizations. Their Web presence includes resources dedicated to conflict management:

http://www.mapnp.org/library/intrpsnl/conflict.htm

Unit Eleven
Small Group Communication
Critical Thinking and Group Decisions

Objectives

Many people report difficulties communicating and working effectively in small groups. Small groups, used properly, can be very efficient problem solvers and decision makers. Group members often do not use proper problem-solving procedures.

- Recognize ineffective small group problem-solving behaviors.
- Adapt dysfunctional behaviors to take advantage of the standard agenda for problem solving.
- Increase your confidence in effective group work by isolating advantages from decision-making guided by problem solving.

Review

The "standard agenda" or "problem-solving sequence" was adapted from John Dewey's suggestions as to how reflective thinking works. Later, group theorists adapted the method. The steps (in various orders, depending on the theorist) include:

- Identify the problem by asking questions of fact, value, and/or policy.
- Analyze the problem by researching its history, causes, effects, symptoms, etc.
- Establish criteria for evaluating potential solutions.
- Generate creative solutions.
- Test solutions with the criteria and select the best solution.
- Implement trial runs of the selected solution(s); evaluate and fine-tune solutions.

Student Learning Guide

Video

Shanenna and Dishari have more than one problem. Not only do they have to prepare a class presentation, but they have to deal with Victoria's schedule, attitude, and plans.

Observations

- Note that even though the three agree (rather tentatively) to do a better presentation, they have not used an efficient procedure for that decision. More than likely, their problem is not solved. One suspects that from Victoria's uninterested response.

- Notice that, between 3 and 6, Victoria actually comes closer to following the standard agenda for problem solving than do her companions.

Next Step

Write dialogue for Shanenna and Dishari that follows the standard agenda for problem solving as a way to convince Victoria that more time and effort should be put into their presentation.

_____

_____

_____

_____

Quiz

1. All group problem solving must use the standard agenda in order to be rational.
    TRUE   FALSE

    _____

2. Theorists order "generating potential solutions" and "establishing criteria for evaluating solutions" in a variety of ways. Why?
   a. Generating criteria before potential solutions can limit creativity and constrain the range of potential solutions.
   b. Generating solutions before establishing criteria can result in many "potential" solutions that are just not practical.
   c. Generating criteria before potential solutions can help groups evaluate potential solutions against real criteria, rather than merely using criteria that prop up decisions that have already been made.
   d. All of the above.

   _____

3. Write the following statement of the problem as an open question:

   "Small groups are better off using an organized set of problem-solving procedures than not using organized steps."

   _____

   _____

Web

The Applied Communication Division of the Southern States Communication Association sponsors a number of Web pages dedicated to putting theory into practice, including pages about small group communication. In the process, they provide information about the standard agenda as problem-solving and decision-making mode:

http://www.roguecom.com/applied/smgp.html

http://www.roguecom.com/applied/StAgenda.html

Unit Twelve
Small Group Communication
Communication and Types of Groups

Objectives

There is no single best way to hold meetings and accomplish group work. Establishing the best procedures depends on the type of group, the nature of the task, and other factors.

- Increase your sensitivity to the variety of factors that determine group type and task dimensions.
- Fine-tune your ability to adjust group meeting procedures flexibly, depending on circumstances.
- Note the damage done when group procedures get at cross-purposes with member needs and preferences.

Review

Group communication occurs for a variety of reasons in a number of settings. The type of group designates, to some degree, the procedures that should occur. Some groups focus on generating ideas (brainstorming), others on personal growth (therapy or catharsis). Groups can share information (learning/study or focus groups) or focus on solving problems and making decisions through work (committees and teams) or politics (parties or movements). Of course, sometimes people function in groups for social and relational reasons (primary groups such as families or social groups), rather than trying to achieve specific goals.

Video

Victoria is late, but she is still not ready to start the meeting. Dishari and Shanenna have good reason to want to get right down to business. Can this group either be fun or do good work?

Observations

- Despite her late arrival, Victoria would like a period of socializing at the start of the meeting. Note how the others cut her off, curtail the social opportunity, and, in the process, set up an adversarial situation.

- From the other perspective, note that Victoria is not sensitive to the implications of being late.

- Victoria suggests the sort of decision making and presentation that Dishari and Shanenna have already ruled out. However, when the three discuss their visions for the presentation, Victoria details reasons for her view, while the other two simply disagree with her and dictate the outcome based on majority rule.

Next Step

- Write dialogue for Dishari and Shanenna that would welcome Victoria, make clear their negative assessment of her late arrival, and yet make room for some socializing at the meeting.

_____

_____

_____

_____

- Write dialogue for Dishari and Shanenna that lays out a constructive process for decision making. They have two decisions to make: First, they have to decide what sort of presentation to make and, second, they have to decide on the procedures they will use for laying out the presentation.

_____

_____

_____

_____

Student Learning Guide

Quiz

1. Primary groups are the decision-making bodies that mean the most to our daily work lives.
    TRUE   FALSE

    _____

2. Focus groups make persuasive announcements and serve as implementation committees for larger groups that have made decisions.
    TRUE   FALSE

    _____

3. Virtual groups, online chat groups, and mailing list groups can benefit from using many of the same procedures as do face-to-face groups.
    TRUE   FALSE

    _____

Web

Carter McNamara, MBA, Ph. D., of Authenticity Consulting, LLC, developed most of the materials found at Web site for The Management Assistance Program for Nonprofits (MAP) in St. Paul, Minnesota. The site, *Free Management Library* (SM), includes excellent resources about the basic nature of groups and how these develop, including numerous subtopics about various types of groups (teams, focus groups, decision-making groups, etc.):

     http://www.mapnp.org/library/

     http://www.mapnp.org/library/grp_skll/theory/theory.htm

Unit Thirteen
Cultural Contexts
Culture in Contexts of Communication

Objectives

Recognizing important cultural differences in contexts is only the first step to effective communication. Interactants must adapt their behaviors appropriately, while maintaining outcome goals. Three dimensions are particularly important.

- Identify where interactants might be placed on a scale between high and low context orientation.
- Identify where interactants might be placed on a masculine vs. feminine scale.
- Identify where interactants might be placed on a individualistic to collectivistic culture scale.
- Suggest behavior adaptations to key differences among interactants.

Review

Culture may be defined as the knowledge, experience, attitudes, beliefs, values, meanings, hierarchies, practices, roles, artifacts, and notions about the universe (space and time) shared by a group of people and handed down from one generation to another.

America is becoming increasingly diverse; communication situations often include a cultural dimension. The greater our differences, the more difficult it is to interpret verbal and nonverbal symbols and to listen accurately to the messages of others and to adapt our messages for others.

Video

Shanenna and Dishari have differing communication styles and do not share some perspectives about the course. However, they are going to work together; we'll see how well.

- Identify where these interactants might be placed on a scale between high and low context orientation.

Shanenna's Cultural Context Orientation

low		high

Dishari's Cultural Context Orientation

```
|-----------------------|-----------------------|
low                                          high
```

- Identify where these interactants might be placed on a masculine vs. feminine scale.

Shanenna's Masculine vs. Feminine Orientation

```
|-----------------------|-----------------------|
masculine                                feminine
```

Dishari's Masculine vs. Feminine Orientation

```
|-----------------------|-----------------------|
masculine                                feminine
```

- Identify where these interactants might be placed on a individualistic to collectivistic culture scale.

Shanenna's Individualistic to Collectivistic Culture Orientation

```
|-----------------------|-----------------------|
individualistic                       collectivistic
```

Dishari's Individualistic to Collectivistic Culture Orientation

```
|-----------------------|-----------------------|
individualistic                       collectivistic
```

Next Step

Suggest behavior adaptations to key differences among interactants. For example, how could Shanenna display sensitivity to Dishari's demonstrated need for agreement? How might Dishari adapt to Shenenna's preference for directness?

_____

_____

_____

_____

Quiz

1. Interactants high in ethnocentricism
    a. strive to understand differences rather than to judge these.
    b. assume that on fundamentals like values and beliefs, all reasonable people are very similar.
    c. seek information from others that might lower uncertainty.
    d. all of the above.

    _____

2. At a model united nations group meeting in which the "representatives" are (actual) ethnic nationals from the represented countries, members who think that the furniture arrangement in the room doesn't much matter and that the group should get right to work rather than enjoying a social hour prior to the meeting are more likely from a:
    HIGH CONTEXT CULTURE   LOW CONTEXT CULTURE

    _____

3. Culture is not a part of communication transactions in which the interactants are from the same ethnic, socio-economic, gender, and racial grouping.
    TRUE   FALSE

    _____

Web

The University of Iowa Department of Communication sponsors an extensive repository of Web links to information on a variety of topics. Links to information about cultural studies are provided along with links to information about gender and race issues as these relate to communication:

http://www.uiowa.edu/~commstud/resources/culturalStudies.html

http://www.uiowa.edu/~commstud/resources/GenderMedia/index.html

Unit Fourteen
Speaking in Public
Organizing Speech Materials

Objectives

Good speeches have clearly identifiable parts: a beginning, middle, and end. Main points, in the body of the speech, are organized according to predictable patterns. This unit will help you to:

- Recognize the value of clearly differentiated parts of public speeches.
- Develop flexibility when selecting and applying organizational patterns for main points.
- Select organizational patterns for main points in accordance with the logics suggested by speech topics and in line with audience expectations.

Review

There are many organizational issues for speeches. This unit covers two: (1) organizing the parts of the speech and (2) organizational patterns for the main points. A third concern, organizing materials within sections (particularly support materials), is covered in "Persuading with Evidence."

A speech should have a clear beginning, middle, and end. These parts are normally represented by the introduction, body, and conclusion of the speech. Within the body of the speech, main points (each divided by related subpoints) organize the content of the presentation.

Main points should be organized in a way that makes sense in light of your treatment of the topic and the expectations of the audience. Patterns include cause and effect, problem solution, time sequence, spatial organization, the motivated sequence, structure-function, comparison-contrast, pro-con, advantages-disadvantages, 5W pattern (who, what, where, when, why), and topical organization.

Video

Michael Whitley's speech about *Laserpaint* is an informative speech given in the championship round of an American Forensics Association national tournament. The introduction, body, and conclusion of the speech are clearly marked. Forensic competitors often combine common patterns to organize main points: you'll note, especially, structure-function and comparison-contrast.

Observations

- Write down what Michael says as transitions between the three major sections of the speech (end of the introduction to start of the body, end of the body to the start of the conclusion).

_____

_____

_____

_____

- List the main points in Michael's speech.

_____

_____

_____

_____

- Identify the ways this main point organization functions as structure-function. Identify the ways this main point organization functions as comparison-contrast.

_____

_____

_____

_____

Next Step

Assuming, roughly, the same content/material used in this speech, reorganize the speech using an alternative organizational pattern for main points. Do not use either structure-function or comparison-contrast. For example, how would you organize this speech following a motivated sequence? The more ways you can reorder the speech, the more you will learn about flexibility with main points. One cannot use every pattern on all topics, but many topics can be organized effectively in a number of ways.

_____

_____

_____

_____

Quiz

1. The introduction is the first part of your speech; therefore, you should work on it first. Once you plan how to get off to a good start, the rest of your speech will fall into place.
    TRUE   FALSE

    _____

2. Organizing your speech provides the following:
    a. The claims in your speech will need support. Organization provides evidence.
    b. Organizational patterns usually make your speech sound structured, constrained, and limited in flexibility.
    c. Speeches with obvious connections and relationships among parts are easier for audiences to follow than are speeches with random order.
    d. All of the above.

    _____

3. The Motivated Sequence organizational pattern
    a. uses the past, present, and future as central theme.
    b. divides the speech into two major sections (in addition to introduction and conclusion).
    c. breaks speeches into self-evident subdivisions.
    d. includes a visualization step.

    _____

Web

Presentations.com features numerous materials for speakers, including a series of articles focused on various approaches to organizing speech materials:

http://www.presentations.com/presentations/creation/organize_archive.jsp

Unit Fifteen
Speaking in Public
Language Choices for Speeches

Objectives

What could be more important to public speaking than the very words that you say?

- Learn to select words that facilitate understanding.
- Learn to select words that increase message impact.
- Learn to avoid word choices and constructions that risk ruining speech impact.

Review

In public speaking, style refers to word choice and arrangement. Speeches combine prepared words with live performance. Selecting and preparing words and phrases carefully and thoroughly can increase communication effectiveness, but what is actually said is sometimes adapted to the needs of the moment. Direct, simple, and clear constructions can help audiences understand the message; vivid, memorable, and pleasing constructions can help "breathe life" into the presentation.

Video

Holly Sisk's topic, "The Need for Correct Hand Washing," persuades about a serious issue within listeners' everyday experience. Her language style upholds the importance of the topic without making it seem overly formal.

Observations

- Note the numerous stylistically interesting choices Ms. Sisk includes throughout her speech.

- For example, early in the introduction, Holly uses "severe gastro-intestinal discomfort," "a new ingredient," and "a new meaning to ordering the number two." Throughout, instances such as these make a telling point and invoke pointed responses from the audience.

- Further, notice that while this speech could be very technical, it is, after all, about bacteria, science, and statistics, Ms. Sisk's language choices ("eewwweeee," "gross," and "wash up, etc.) keep the speech on a level appropriate to laypeople.

Next Step

Write five sentences describing the poisoning incident in Minnesota that Holly details at the start of the speech. Use one of these five elements of figurative language in each sentence. Write as though you were going to deliver each sentence in a speech on this topic.

Hyperbole:

_____

_____

Metaphor:

_____

_____

Personification:

_____

_____

Simile:

_____

_____

Rhetorical Question:

_____

_____

Quiz

1. Decisions about style should favor "fancy-sounding" words and relatively complex constructions so that the audience gets the impression that you really know what you are talking about.
    TRUE   FALSE

    _____

2. Decisions about style should favor "everyday-sounding" words and constructions so that the audience hears you speak as you do in normal conversations.
    TRUE   FALSE

    _____

3. Changes in American society, especially increases in the use of slang, vulgar, and offensive expressions on television and in films, have made the use of these informal ways of speaking acceptable in public speaking situations.
    TRUE   FALSE

    _____

Web

The "Forest of Rhetoric," *silva rhetoricae,* is an online guide dedicated by Dr. Gideon Burton of Brigham Young University to the hundreds of terms naming figures of speech. The site also provides instruction about many aspects of style:

http://humanities.byu.edu/rhetoric/silva.htm

Unit Sixteen
Informative Speaking
Better Understanding Via Informative Speech

Objectives

Informative speeches function by adjusting new information in ways that effectively increase listener knowledge.

- Note the importance of specific purpose statements in informative speeches. Although informative speeches may contain information that is "news" to listeners, information should not be packaged as a "surprise." The audience should be able to predict what information the speaker will cover and how she/he will go about it.
- Appreciate that although information can lead to new ways of thinking, informative speeches are not designed for persuasive outcomes.
- Critique flaws in main point patterning when these threaten understanding.

Review

Informative speeches increase listener knowledge. These can be about objects, processes, events, people, and ideas/concepts. Informatives can be speeches of description, definition, or demonstration.

Good informative speeches bring audiences information they don't already know, but do so without overwhelming the audience by focusing on the information and by relating new information to old. Informative speakers adjust the level of the information so the audience can follow, understand, and remember it, and they underscore the usefulness of the information.

Informative speakers often use audio/visual aides to help the audience visualize aspects of the speech; when they present support materials, they document the sources of their information carefully.

Video

Michael Lynch carries two main points in his speech. He previews these as part of a very explicit specific purpose statement. Note the informative nature of this presentation.

Observations

- Note that Mr. Lynch's main point preview (just before 2) is flawed. Although he says that he will talk about (a) two new teaching methods (b) government programs for progressive learning and (c) changes in the future of education, his third point is actually covered in his conclusion rather than in a main point.

- Mr. Lynch primarily uses description and explanation to inform his audience. Note how, at 5, he supports his description of collaborative learning with a story reported in *Time* magazine.

Next Step

- Rewrite the statement of specific purpose and the main point preview in a way that better specifies and clarifies the structure of this speech.

_____

_____

_____

- Indicate places in his speech that Mr. Lynch could (or should) have used additional evidence in support of his descriptions.

_____

_____

- Assess the effectiveness of this speaker's attempts to bolster his credibility on this topic. Note, particularly, his early references to his personal experience.

_____

_____

Quiz

1. Speech techniques are not of much use to informative speakers: If the information is really important and "true," it will, generally, impact the audience merely because it is so.

    TRUE   FALSE

    _____

2. The purpose of informative speaking is to increase audience understanding. To that end,
    a. speakers should present a lot of very complex information,because listeners will find this informative.
    b. speakers should present as many facts as they can fit into the available timeframe.
    c. citing sources for information is not as important in informative speaking as it is in persuasive speaking.
    d. the level of abstraction at which one speaks must be adjusted to that at which the audience can best comprehend the material.

    _____

3. You've done some basic research on your topic, but the speech is due tomorrow and you need to rehearse it, so you are writing, rather than doing more research. You don't fully understand the entire subject, but you have some specific information about the part on which you are speaking. You didn't note the sources, so you don't plan citing the evidence directly. You aren't sure that the point you are making is true, but the speech you've written sounds good enough as you rehearse it. This situation raises major questions about:

    _____

    _____

Web

You are most likely learning about informative speaking in a speech communication or communication class. Other academic disciplines also have interests in informative speaking. For example, the fact that one often writes the speech before delivering it finds teachers of English or writing interested in informative speaking.

The Writing Center at Colorado State University provides extensive coverage of the process of preparing informative speeches:

http://writing.colostate.edu/references/speaking/infomod/

Unit Seventeen
Persuasive Speaking
Setting Goals for Persuasive Speeches

Objectives

Persuasive speaking requires an artful mix of materials and approaches. Effective persuasive speakers "surround" their audiences with solid motivations for change. Increase your ability to use each of the three kinds of persuasive materials:

- Bolster your credibility in topic-relevant ways.
- Effective methods for giving good reasons, particularly via the presentation of evidence and source citation.
- Emotional appeals that engage the audience's feelings without alienating listeners.

Review

Persuasive speaking attempts to reinforce or change listeners by getting them to adopt, discontinue, avoid, or continue an attitude, belief, value, or behavior. Effective persuasive speakers establish their credibility on issues, convince the audience that their claims are reasonable, and appeal to the emotions of the audience as ways to induce change. Persuasive speeches deal with questions of fact, definition, policy, and value. Listener involvement in the topic is important, as is the degree to which the speech goal is in line with audience members' current thinking and their perceived need to change.

Video

Heath Rainbolt's speech about body image distortion is made particularly persuasive by his high personal involvement. However, note his strong use of organization, the presentation of lots of credible evidence, and the speech's telling emotional appeals. Although he could, Heath doesn't depend on his credibility alone.

Observations

- Note the way that Mr. Rainbolt uses problem-solution organization for his main points.

- Make note of the numerous times (and ways) that Heath includes audience members by using the terms, "us," "we," and "you." This is a speech about the audience, though they would not normally think so.

- Perhaps the most effective persuasive element comes just after 4–the point at which Mr. Rainbolt presents evidence implicating people free from eating disorders in the large issue of body image distortion. This makes the speech apply to all audience members. Detail the way that he makes this artful connection.

_____

_____

_____

Next Step

Write a brief outline for this speech, changing the organization pattern to the motivated sequence and removing the personal involvement element (the speaker no longer has an eating disorder). Note the changes that would be required if this were to remain an effective speech.

_____

_____

_____

_____

Quiz

1. If speakers are persuasive enough, they can convince audiences to change their fundamental values as a result of a given speech.
    TRUE   FALSE

    _____

2. Heath's specific purposes are to examine body image distortion by looking at its definition, it's impact on society, and ways to beat it. The goal of his speech focuses on
    a. question of fact.
    b. question of value.
    c. question of policy.

    _____

3. Which kinds of motivations does Heath use?
    a. Dissonance
    b. Needs
    c. Fear
    d. all of the above

    _____

Web

Allyn & Bacon's *Communication Studies* Web site features an interactive activity titled "Persuasive Speaking on Legislative Topics." The purpose of this activity is to use government documents on the World Wide Web to gather information about a topic that is under consideration by lawmakers:

http://www.abacon.com/pubspeak/exercise/congtop.html

Unit Eighteen
Persuasive Speaking
Persuading With Evidence

Objectives

Informative and persuasive speeches benefit from the presentation of evidence that supports claims audience members may find questionable.

- Identify the claim-evidence structure in speeches to "catch" unsupported claims or insufficient support.
- Recognize a variety of evidence types and consider factors indicating the quality and usability of support factors.
- Learn to cite sources accurately, efficiently, and effectively.

Review

Speeches benefit from the presentation of material that audiences find acceptable as support for messages. Speakers do well to identify each claim of fact, definition, value, or policy that they make and use audience analysis to decide if the claim is already acceptable (a taken-for-granted). Speakers should provide support for any claims that are not agreed to.

Audiences must understand the material and find the information credible; they must understand how the information connects to the speaker's claims (find it relevant), and they must think that the speaker presents enough good reasons for them to accept a given claim.

Whenever support that is not common knowledge is offered, accurate source citations should be used both to bolster the effect of the evidence and to enable the audience to judge the quality of the material. Types of support include illustrations, descriptions and explanations, definitions, analogies, statistics, expert testimony, and physical evidence.

Video

Ben Lohman's speech about identity theft (name fraud) can only be successful if he convinces the audience that the problem is significant in both scope and impact. Note how he uses evidence to persuade listeners to be concerned based on evidence indicating that they are not immune from the problem. Also, each support is properly cited.

Observations

- List the four instances of supporting materials that Mr. Lohman uses in the introduction of his speech. What type of evidence is each?

_____

_____

_____

_____

- Note the oral citations Ben uses for his evidence. What elements are stressed?

_____

_____

_____

_____

- What are the most prominent types of support used in this speech?

_____

_____

_____

_____

Next Step

Outline the material covered in the first main point of this speech, especially noting the relationships between claims and the data that supports these.

_____

_____

_____

_____

Quiz

1. Oral citations for materials drawn from Web sites should include the URL (Web address) where the material was found.
    TRUE   FALSE

    _____

2. Celebrities make good sources for expert testimony
    a. because they are well-known, regardless of the subject on which they are quoted.
    b. when they are quoted regarding subjects within their expertise (actors on acting, doctors on medicine, basketball players on basketball, etc.).
    c. only when they are not speaking about the kind of work they do; too much bias results when celebrities speak about their own expertise.
    d. none of the above.

    _____

3. It is not necessary to cite sources for information and support when

    _____

Web

The Cornell School of Law sponsors *The Legal Information Institute* (*LII*), a site often identified as the most linked to Web resource in the field of law. Although using evidence in public speaking does not have to follow laws that apply in court settings, learning about how evidence is handled in the American system of justice helps speakers fine-tune their abilities to manage support materials. LII provides a number of links to resources about the use of evidence:

http://www.law.cornell.edu/topics/evidence.html

CORRELATION GRID CONNECTING
CHAPTERS TO MODULES

#	Concept	Beebe, et al. Comm	DeVito, Essentials, 4/e	DeVito, Human Comm, 9/e	Seiler & Beall Communication 5/e
1	Irreversible Process	Chapter 1	Chapter 1	Unit 2	Chapter 1
2	Self-concept	Chapter 2	Chapter 2	Unit 6	Chapter 3
3	Self-esteem	Chapter 2	X	Unit 6	Chapter 3
4	Self-disclosure	Chapter 8	Chapter 2	Unit 6	Chapter 13
5	Perception Checking	Chapter 2	Chapter 3	Unit 4	Chapter 2
6	Denotation-Conotation	Chapter 3	Chapter 5	Unit 7	Chapter 4
7	Abstraction	Chapter 3	Chapter 5	Unit 18	Chapter 4
8	Nonverbal	Chapter 4	Chapter 6	Unit 8	Chapter 5
9	Gender in Language	Chapter 6	Chapters 4 & 5	Units 5 & 7	Chapter 3
10	Conflict	Chapter 8	Chapter 7	Unit 11	Chapter 14
11	Group Decision Making	Chapter 10	Chapter 10	Unit 13	Chapter 16
12	Types of Groups	Chapter 9	Chapter 10	Unit 13	Chapter 15
13	Cultural contexts	Chapter 6	Chapter 1	Units 1 & 19	Chapter 2
14	Organization	Chapter 12	Chapter 12	Unit 16	Chapter 9
15	Style	Chapter 13	Chapter 13	Unit 17	Chapters 11 & 12
16	Informative	Chapter 14	Chapter 14	Unit 18	Chapter 11
17	Persuasive	Chapter 15	Chapter 15	Unit 19	Chapter 12
18	Evidence	Chapter 11	Chapters 12 & 14	Unit 16	Chapters 11 & 12

NOTES

NOTES

NOTES

NOTES

NOTES

NOTES

NOTES

NOTES

NOTES

NOTES

NOTES

NOTES

NOTES

NOTES

NOTES